Male Invert

Edward Penny

chipmunkapublishing
the mental health publisher

All rights reserved, no part of this publication may be reproduced by any means, electronic, mechanical photocopying, documentary, film or in any other format without prior written permission of the publisher.

>Published by
>Chipmunkapublishing
>United Kingdom

http://www.chipmunkapublishing.com

Copyright © Edward Penny 2025

Hello and welcome to these pages!

This is my personal account of my gender identity and my experience with gender, based on introspection and the things I have been through in my life

It is very much a personal account and that is how I want people to take it, even if it may somehow contribute to the field, and I think it would be good if it did.

I think that what goes for me could also go for others too, hence me sharing this.

I wish I could send this book back in time and give it to my past self!

And I hope what I write won't make anyone angry or pissed off because what I write is what I authentically believe! – I know that with sex, gender, and sexuality passions can run high and that people take things personally!

It is my hope that this book may in some way help others, who are still trying to figure out their own gender identity

No matter how you ultimately chose to live your life I hope this book will be of some use and that it will help you make informed decisions

Maybe it's for you and maybe it isn't but I hope you will at least read it

I have written it as I did not feel as though there was a gender identity that fitted me, that matched up to who and what I am, I had no identity that fitted me – that I could inhabit and call my own.

I think it would be really cool if people out there choose to go down the same path I did but I'm not here to sell any one single solution, I'm only telling my story, and providing my perspective on things

I have published this book with a specialist Mental Health publisher, so there is a bit of an emphasis on wellbeing and positive mental health – happiness, basically!

This is the second version of this book

Version 2.0

After I signed off on the release of Version 1.0 I initially regretted much of what I said and had my publishers withdraw it from the global book trade, pending major revisions

I could no longer stand by what I wrote, and what I wrote did not represent me or my views

It did not represent the thoughts in my head nor the feelings in my heart, so I pulled it

I want my books to be paper (or digital) extensions of me – a record of my thoughts and feelings

Version 1 did not represent me…

Version 2.0 is also a much, much, much better book!

Even if I do say so myself…

Here is Version 2.0:

It was originally called "A New Gender Regime" and the aim was to provide an alternative model for humankind to use in order to better conceptualize sex and gender, according to the actual realities of sex and gender

It was a new framework for ordering our society, for people to do sex and gender

However, I soon regretted this and considered that old title somewhat grandiose and big-headed. So instead I changed the focus – focusing on my own personal sexuality and gender identity as well as a source of ideas for to how to better think about sex and gender in general

The aim of this book is to contribute to the discussion, to help society better understand sex and gender – not to storm in and instil some new order – some new regime.

I want to be heard, that's all. I don't want to be obeyed, or anything like that. I have no interest in being a public figure, that is not my business. I did not write this book to be an ego vehicle.

It is here to be helpful and bring clarity, not to take over the world!

Allow me to introduce who I am and what I identify as being

I will do this quickly right now, but will go into greater detail further into the book, explaining exactly what I mean by the term I am about to use

Basically: I identify **as a <u>Male Invert</u>**

An Invert who is male!

Which is any male person who self-consciously identifies more with traits and vibes that are more feminine than masculine, whilst presenting to the world as a man – as "him" and "he" but who identifies with feminine gender traits and feminine vibes

I am male and I identify more with femininity than masculinity whilst identifying as a man (rather than a woman) – hence according to this understanding I am a Male Invert

In its original use, in the Victorian era, the term was used to refer to homosexuals. However, in the way that I use it the term refers to masculine women and feminine men, regardless of their sexual preferences. I offer it as a gender identity, not as some sexual orientation. In language, the meanings of terms and words can shift over time.

To identify as a Male Invert is for a man to say that they are more feminine, as opposed to more masculine. But who chooses to carry on living as a man, without changing their pronouns or manner of dress, etc.

However: There is a difference between a man who is more feminine than masculine and yet identifies simply as a man and a person who is more feminine than masculine and who explicitly self-consciously identifies as a Male Invert and who adopts that as their gender identity

To be a Male Invert is to be a self-identified member of a certain social group. Not all males who are feminine would identify as Male Inverts, either because they don't want to or they've never heard of it. So, not all feminine males are Male Inverts. "Male Invert" is a thing that a feminine man can identify with though.

The other thing that a feminine male can do is to live as a Transwoman. Not my way, but a way.

It is a type of self-declared personal identity. It is something that a person identifies as, rather than a label that is attached to them by others. The way I see it, a person is only a Male Invert if they personally identify as one, regardless of how others may view them, or classify them.

And of course, there are Female Inverts too. And I think that much of what goes for Male Inverts also goes for Female Inverts.

But this book focuses on what it means to be a Male Invert. But hopefully Female Inverts will find it useful too!

My point being: identification as a Male Invert has to come from the person involved, it is not a label for others to attach

However, there is nothing wrong with saying to someone "have you ever considered yourself a Male Invert?" – so long as you don't try to argue or convince them into identifying as one or constantly badger them.

But yeah, if you already know them and are on somewhat intimate terms then there can be no harm in asking, no harm in raising the issue and making them aware of it

I believe that most Trans-Women are feminine people who could identify as a Male Invert if they felt differently. I will go over the differences and similarities between Transwomen and Male Inverts later in this book. But I'll say this now: I think that they are a similar set of people who have different responses to the same set of circumstances.

Male Inverts may experience Gender Dysphoria. I know I did. But the difference between them and Transwomen is how they cope with Gender Dysphoria. Those who become Transwomen do so as a solution to Gender Dysphoria. If that works for them then all power to them, but for others doing that does not feel like much of a solution

The solution to Gender Dysphoria for a self-identified Male Invert is to realise that feminine does not automatically mean "female" – that not all females are feminine, and not all feminine people are female – and that it is legitimate and not non-sensical to be a feminine male. That being that way is not a problem that needs some kind of solution.

For a Male Invert, a way of dealing with Gender Dysphroia is to say to yourself "those feelings – although legitimate and reasonable – don't stand up to analysis" and changing the definition of things in your brain

Your sub-conscious needs to be on side though, as do your emotions

It is a thing you get into both as a conscious commitment and on the basis of what your instincts tell you about how reality works, for me both reason and emotion guided me to become a Male Invert

Being an ordinary male and being a Transwoman were not options for me, they did not feel right for me, so I went down the Male Invert road.

It felt right to me, and it made sense to me. So I did it.

It basically amounts to thinking yourself out of Gender Dysphoria, by altering the mental furniture in your head. It involves re-wiring yourself and rejecting all of the programs society and culture has installed in your mind:

Both the dominant, hegemonic gender constructs but also other, alternative ones

For me, the decision to identify as a Male Invert involved rejecting other paradigms, other narratives. Male Invert was the only option for me.

It's all about living as your true self. If your true self wears skirts and calls themselves "she" then that's cool, and if they'd rather wear trousers and call themselves "he" then that is also cool

We are all individuals and what works as a solution for some won't work for others, humanity is gloriously diverse!

For me, consciously choosing to identify as a Male Invert involved saying "fuck sex and fuck gender, this is the way for me"

I don't want to be a gender identity; I want to be a well-rounded human being who (like all people) just so happens to have a gender identity!

That's why I'm a Male Invert, but in becoming a Male Invert I had to reject the option of becoming a Transwoman, and I have my reasons for doing that. But I'm not saying those reasons are for everyone, because clearly they're not!

I don't see any tablet of stone that says "if you are feminine then your authentic self is truly a woman" nor any that says "if you are masculine then your authentic self is truly a man" – Male Invert and Female Invert are both options for feminine males and masculine females.

Just a quick notice about this book: Sometimes I capitalise terms like Transwoman and sometimes I don't. The same goes for Male Invert and male invert. Please, do not read too much into my capitalisation! I did not write this book from start to finish; its construction was fairly modular. Different paragraphs on the same page may have been written months apart. And I am not working according to any consistent style guide. So please be patient and don't take offense – because none is intended!

As a Male Invert I consider myself to be almost in the same category as trans-women, the difference being is that I present as being a man, not a woman

But beyond that, I believe we have much in common

It's just that we've gone down different paths – made different lifestyle choices to reflect our different senses of what our authentic selves are like

And yes – I have made a firm personal decision to live as a man. That is a conclusion I came to after a great many years of Gender Dysphoria, which I never shared with anyone – not a soul. I did not have one "Eureka!" moment or anything like that, that's just how I developed over a number of years, with the issue always present – towards the back of my mind!

The gears of my mind grinded slowly and surely – they did not spin madly!

I have a history of gender dysphoria and identify more with women than with most men and I am sympathetic towards trans-woman

It's just that I'd never want to be one – and I will discuss that later in this book

Hence I'm not one

The difference is in how we choose to live our lives and how we want to be treated

Had things only been a little bit more different maybe I would have become one? Who knows! What if Hitler had captured the British Expeditionary Force in Dunkirk in 1940? I have no idea…

Anyway, I consider myself "Queer" and I am a male who is mostly attracted to other men

And I know that not all people who could call themselves "Queer" like that term, but I personally have no problem with it, and I think Queer people should try and be supportive of each other

I think minorities should stick together

Although I support the LGBT movement I much prefer to call myself "homosexual", rather than "gay" because I believe that "gay" is a social construct, a social role, a social status. Whereas "homosexual" is simply a sexual orientation. A thing that is a natural part of people.

When I call myself "homosexual" I feel like much more of an individual than when I call myself "gay" – "homosexual" does what it says on the tin whereas "gay" has all manner of connotations attached to it, some much nicer than others

For instance, it makes me think of men cruising in public park for sex or wearing nothing but leather trousers with the butt cut out dancing on the dancefloor (to techno music) of a subterranean night-club. Those things are not my scene! That's not the type of person I am but I support those who are that type of person. And yes, I know those are stupid stereotypes. That's why I invoked them!

I also don't like the term "sodomite". Not all sodomites are gay men, and not all gay men are sodomites. And I personally am not into any of that.

But yes, if you were to ask me "are you gay?" I would say "yes", even though if you were to ask me "what is your sexual orientation" I would say "homosexual" rather than "gay"

I feel much more comfortable limiting my identification to being simply "homosexual" however I support the rights of gay people and same-sex couples and am on the side of LGBT liberation and equality

I am a big believer in everyone mattering, everyone being equal

And I believe that people should get to choose to be whatever type of person they truly are. If you'd be happier and more true to yourself as a Transwoman then go and be a Transwoman. If you'd feel happier and more true to yourself as a Male Invert then go and be a Male Invert. We all have the right to choose.

For some feminine men that may mean presenting as a woman but that's a big leap and not one that has to be made, I am a feminine man but I have zero interest in changing my sex presentation to reflect that, I see no tension between "feminine" and "man" and I don't feel abnormal or anything like that – yet for a great many years I felt nagging and persistent Gender Dysphoria, it was less furniture in my mind and more the colour of paint on the walls, and the style of curtains around the windows and the choice of carpet

I associated being Feminine with being Female and that simple confusion was I believe the source of my Gender Dysphoria, rather than any actual mismatch between the gender of my brain and the sex of my body

It impinged on me living my life in a happy and fulfilling way

I support trans people. And I mean real people, not the awful stereotypes people have of them. I feel solidarity with them and judge them as individuals based on the quality of their character.

However: I feel that the activities and views of some members of the trans-movement – trans-activists if you will – are absurd, unjust, and socially (and sometimes even personally) harmful.

But that's only *certain activists* and *certain parts* of that movement

But the point is: I don't support any cause just because it is advocated by Trans activists, things have to be consistent with my own moral sense too, for me to support them

My point being: I am on the side of trans people however I don't support every single thing that is done in the name of trans people or in the name of trans liberation

Mostly because other people matter too.

I have standards: I don't like absurdity, injustice, and harm – be it social or personal. Even when it comes from groups with whom I feel empathy and otherwise support.

When planning this book, my main thrust was going to be "why I'm not trans" but I thought that would be a bit negative and could be interpreted as transphobic and the aim of this book is to advocate Male Invert as a gender identity – not to belittle or pick apart the Trans identity.

I am here to build up "Male Invert", not teardown "Transwoman". The two are alternative choices but not in any conflict, what goes for one person may not go for another.

It's not a competition! They are not rival groups!

There are some things that go on that I don't think are cool and I want no part in supporting such things. I believe that it is possible to be a friend and ally to transpeople whilst still being opposed to these various things. Being a friend and ally does not need blind and unconditional support, no matter what. And it most certainly does not involve laying aside your own moral sensibilities and concerns.

And I know that the things I am about to list cannot be pinned upon all Transwomen, I'm just giving them as examples to the fact that my willingness to support society accommodating their demands has limits. And yes, I have gleaned these examples mostly from the sewer press that likes to get itself very excited about things

These are some of the things that I am not cool with:

- ❖ Feminine male children being labelled as being somehow "truly" female and being given hormones to feminise them or even surgery. As little kids, who probably still believe in Santa Claus… (more on this later)

- ❖ Transwomen prisoners with penises being put in women's prisons amongst a female prison population

- ❖ Transwomen athletes beating female athletes in sporting competitions. Taking the piss big time. Utterly shameless cheating.

- ❖ A university professor being hounded out of her job (by people in balaclavas) for objecting to people with penises going into the female changing rooms at the swimming pool

- ❖ Men who identify as women denouncing *lesbians* who refuse to sleep with them as "transphobic" and worthy of society's scorn, and personal ruin – as though them not wanting to sleep with them is a hate crime! I don't think this happens often, but it has happened.

❖ The whole "punch a TERF" meme. Violence against women. How lovely!!

These things are clearly unacceptable, by any reasonable standard. And I think those involved with these get a free pass from the liberal community that they would not otherwise receive

And yes, stories like this are used to mobilise reactionary and social conservative opinion, they make good clickbait

And I think they distract from the real issues: namely advancing the interests of the working-class at the expense of the capitalists. That's the struggle I'm most interested in, not against or for various other things, to me those matter but are only of secondary importance

And for the record, I think being a male and calling yourself a "she" and dressing in women's clothes is totally cool and a legitimate way for one to live one's life

And yes, I know that they don't need my approval to do what they do! I'm just stating my position on this, that's all.

I will not let the feelings of indignation these points inspire inside of me turn into a problem with real-life trans individuals and the trans community at large. I disapprove of the above absurdities, injustices, and excesses. Not of any one person or any wider group of people.

I'm a man and I don't want to be associated with everything that particular groups of men do! – and I don't call people having problems with certain male individuals anti-man. When it has nothing to do with being a man and everything about being obnoxious. But I will not identify the groups I'm thinking of, not here.

And as you will see, a bit part of my personal ideology is the idea that people should be treated as individuals, unique individuals – not according to their membership of any category or group. That's one of the ways in which I try to live my life!

That's why to me a Transwoman is more than a man in a dress. If they were just a man in a dress then they wouldn't be a Transwoman. There has to be certain things going on in their head. And their heart and soul too, perhaps.

It is a social status as much as a personal characteristic.

In Version 1 I did let those feeling colour my judgment and the tone of my book, which was not a good thing for me to have done.

There are excesses, but excesses of an otherwise legitimate movement which I think should be accommodated to a considerable degree, until it encroaches on the interests, rights, and wishes of others.

The legitimate interests, rights and wishes of others, might I add

I believe that trans people should be accommodated far as decently possible. However I do not think that certain measures such as only XX people being allowed to compete in women's events are in anyway "transphobic" or wrong

In boxing we have weight categories – segregating boxing based on their sex chromosomes is no more far-fetched than segregating it on how heavy the competitors are.

It would not be a fair fight were a flyweight be pitched against a super-heavyweight in the ring. Likewise, males fighting females in boxing would also be wrong.

Different biology = different status

For instance age is a biological status that affects social status! – e.g. "child", "teenager", "young adult", "middle-aged", "elderly" etc. – and nobody has any control over that

Yet being in a certain age group does not confer superior status, or lower status. They are distinctions, yes. But not stratifications of status, of worth.

To demand that everyone always conforms to your every single demand is childish. As is getting upset and angry when things don't constantly go your way. The aim should be for everyone to live together and co-exist, not for your particular party to always get its way, over other groups

If words are weapons, then the last thing I want to do is to help arm objectionable people to the teeth, the type of people who bullied me a lot at school for being different and a non-masculine boy with extravagant hair.

I want nothing to do with the haters. I am a Male Invert and as a teenager I was given hell for that, even though at the time I did not explicitly identify as a Male Invert.

If you are a NAZI who is reading this for ammunition against trans people or LGBT then this book is not for you

I hope people will forgive me my past excesses. I regret them deeply. I want to be a force for peace and love, I want to unite and bring people together, not cause discord and enmity between different groups, especially towards vulnerable minorities

And I think Male Inverts are a minority group.

But I have moved on, I am no longer that person. The way I see it, I had to go through all that to move on, in what I believe will be the correct direction for me.

For me a stage on my path to becoming a self-identified Male Invert involved a rejection of the Transwoman identity and the Trans community and world view as well. I had to go through those things not being for me in order to arrive at my current destination. But now I'm here I have nothing against Trans.

It's just not right for me, that's all.

I did not make the leap of becoming a transwoman for various reasons, and I am very glad that I didn't. And in the end, I ended up feeling much better about myself. I am more happy as a Male Invert than I ever was as being simply a man.

By acquiring the Male Invert Consciousness my Gender Dysphoria was expelled

Well, I think I starved it of (mental) nutrients so shrivelled, died, and then dropped off

Perhaps in a parallel universe I did go down the Trans road?

I greatly empathise with trans-women. That's one of the reasons why the certain injustices I listed earlier get to me so much, it feels like they are coming from my people, even though I am not in the trans camp. I do however identify as LGBT.

There is a group called the LGB Alliance, who say that the struggles and challenges faced by gays/lesbians/bisexuals are distinct from those face by the trans community and I think there may be something in that and that they might have a point

However, I personally don't mind being classed as being in the same broad category as the trans people. Are we not all human? I have been to pride events in the past, and by doing that I was registering my support for the dignity and acceptance of trans people as well as for the LGB people.

Transphobia and Homophobia are two things that I am against.

I consider myself a trans ally but that does not equate to issuing a blank moral cheque to anything whatsoever that trans activists may want or actually becoming one of that group.

For instance, a guy who only comes in at fifth of sixth place when competing against male athletes and then starts competing against female athletes and then comes first every time is a cheat who does not deserve any titles or medals. It's as simple as that.

And also, I need to point this out: **Male Invert does not mean "homosexual"** – you can be a

Male Invert and be of any sexual persuasion: gay, straight, bi, pan – whatever! It just so happens that I'm more attracted to men than to women. But that's very much a separate issue to my gender identity.

Male Invert is a gender identity, not a sexuality. Just like how Transwomen can sleep with either males or females and still be Transwomen.

Anyway, that's how I feel about all that right now. Maybe things will change in the future?

Maybe some people would disagree with this, but the thing is, I don't think **anyone** should be mistreated or discriminated against – including the trans people. But that doesn't mean that a person with a penis should be locked up in a prison alongside women or compete in (for instance) martial arts or athletics against people with vaginas. Those two scenarios are clearly unjust and wrong. To anyone who thinks even one bit about the interests of other people.

I think that trying to accommodate differences and trying to get different types of people to live together harmoniously is a very Feminine trait. The Feminine way!!!

There has to be limits. In society we should all strive to co-exist and not come into conflict with each other. It's all about respect. And respect goes two ways; it is a thing you can demand and also a thing that you have an obligation to honour when it comes to others. It's a game of give and take!

Freedom has limits and it is not reasonable to demand that your rights and demands always trump those of others. There has to be limits on personal freedom – and I believe those limits end where the other people's freedoms begin.

Supporting the rights of a minority and sticking up for them does not equate to accepting every single demand of self-proclaimed "activists". Other people have rights and needs too and we need to be civil. It is not reasonable or mature to demand that everything you want to be automatically granted and to then play the "-phobia" card when it isn't.

For a long time I lived under the constant nagging dissatisfaction of Gender Dysphoria, but I never made much of a noise about it. But I did think it would be better if I was female. But never considered going trans to be an option. The way I saw it, that would make my situation even worse and would solve nothing. At least for me.

It would have in no way been a solution for me. It would have made things worse.

However, I managed to finally resolve it. I thought my way out of it. I made myself believe that those feelings needn't be felt and that I could live happily and authentically as who I already was.

I re-programmed myself, I re-wired my brain. By thinking about stuff consciously, and then letting it stew on the back burner, slowly cooking away on the back burner whilst I battled with depression and schizophrenia. But it was always there, always happening, always going on.

And that **FOR ME** those feelings turned out to be irrational. And that there was nothing miserable about my condition.

I believe that by identifying as a Male Invert I have hit upon my true, authentic identity. I have discovered **what** I am and by doing that I am now happy with **who** I am. That's me. I'm not just a man and I'm not a Transwoman. I'm a Male Invert. That's me. I found out what I was, and I started living and thinking according to that.

Adopting that identity made me make sense to myself.

We all have a gender identity! – it is a part of being human!

Now, another note on this book:

As you may have noticed, this book doesn't have chapters or paragraphs

Not in the traditional way!

It is a flow

I don't like full-stops either, at least not at the end of a section of text

So I'm not going to use them like that

I don't care if you don't like it this is how I roll

If you want, you can always get a pen and add full-stops at the end of every line in this book that should have one?

The previous version of this book was more traditional; its content was presented in conventional paragraphs which were organized into chapters

All very bourgeois!

Version 1 of the original book started off with my own experiences of sex and gender, that was Chapter 1 and I stand by the contents of that chapter

Chapter 2 was my understanding of sex and gender, and I stand by most of that although not the bit about my own sex and gender – that has always been somewhat subject to change!

The tricky one was Chapter 3 where I proposed a new "gender regime" – a new way of society to do sex and gender based on an understanding of sex and gender provided in Chapter 2

The end of this book is now very different to how it was originally

But then I totally re-did this book and made it about being a Male Invert rather than a guide to some new way of doing sex and gender

If you pick this book up and read it from cover to cover then the concept of "Male Invert" as I understand it will exist in your head and will influence your thoughts!

But I still share some of my ideas about how we as a society should do gender and sex – although these have changed a bit since Version 1.0

I am open to dialogue, about how best we humans can best organize our society, so that everyone is satisfied with the arrangements. That is a conversation that I want to be a part of.

Transwomen are certainly demonised in certain right-wing media outlets, and I don't want to have any part in that, and they make an easy target

We should punch up, not down and having a go at trans-women is punching down although that doesn't mean that the conduct of the trans-movement and trans-activists should not be questioned or challenged – they should be, to the same extent as the conduct of everyone else

In a free society, nobody can expect a free pass and reasonably expect to be totally and unconditionally accommodated. Because that happening would impinge on the liberties, demands, and interests of others.

Anyway, a person who is majorly obsessed with the sex and gender issues is not the kind of person I want to be, and in this life we all get to choose what type of person we become, and I don't want to be obsessed with sex and gender, and I certainly don't want to be a transphobe!

I think that some gay people only have their homosexuality as a personality, I've met a few people like that, they are vacuous and shallow, nothing to them. What's the point in them? I would never want to be like that!

I could name some celebrities who have fallen into that trap, but I don't want to give such people the oxygen of publicity, but they are stupid people whom I find tedious and repulsive. So let's leave it at that.

I like all the transwomen I know, both online and "IRL" (in real life) and I know two transmen online too, who are wonderful people whom I like and respect, I think they are both taking Testosterone right now

So I base my view of transwomen on the reality of those individuals, not on clickbait outraged scare stories on in The Daily Mail or places like that – the sewer press

If I had to choose between the lives of the transpeople I know and the editorial staff of the Daily Mail in some kind of balloon debate ("there are five people in the basket of a hot-air balloon and the balloon is about to crash into the ocean and you have to throw one person overboard to stop it crashing into the sea so that it can gain altitude, who do you throw out and why?") then I would throw out the Daily Mail people to stop the balloon crashing.

Every time.

Peter Hitchens and Alison Boshoff too!

If you want another reason to not like the Daily Mail, go and Google "hooray for the black shirts"

I wouldn't want to be a trans person myself, although I have a lot of respect for them, to do what they do takes confidence, it's a big bold step to make, very brave I'd say

And let it be said: as a man I am accepting of transmen into male groups and spaces – but we will get into all that later on!

I am a Trans-Inclusive Male.

I am happy to embrace transmen as brothers, if they are seriously committed to being transmen, on the basis of Gender Dysphoria and their Gender identity

This is the thrust of my story: I eventually thought my way out of my Gender Dysphoria, without becoming trans and without oppressing and fighting back my true self

In the end, I sorted myself out – and not all people can say that about themselves

I didn't oppress my feelings; I channelled them into something new: the identity of Male Invert

And as a self-identified Male Invert I got over Gender Dysphoria, I felt authentic, and I made sense to myself – in ways that I did not before

Here's a question for the age: Can a woman have a penis?

I think "woman" is both a biological status but also a social role – so in one sense I don't think it is possible for a man to become a woman (biology) but in another it is perfectly possible (social) – but I will go over that later

Some things just aren't "Yes" or "No" answers

So, can a woman have a penis? I know this may sound like a cop-out, but that depends on if you mean "woman" socially or biologically. If biologically, then no. If socially, then yes. But we will go into all that later.

And I know, it is likely transwomen don't think of it in terms of them *becoming* a woman, to them they are a type of woman already. According to their sex/gender schematics. I get that, and I understand that subtlety: that it is the societal status that changes to affirm the realities of the individual as they already are

As you will see I operate a distinction between physically a woman and socially a woman and I make a distinction between "sex" and "sex presentation"

(I will explore all that later)

Since for me the problem of Gender Dysphoria could not be solved by becoming a transwoman I had to find other ways out, and for me I found that by contemplating the realities of sex and gender until I realised that it's a non-issue and not a big deal or anything to get upset about

And once I realised that a weight was lifted off my shoulders and everything felt much better

And then I embraced a new identity: Male Invert

In my studies at university I came across the Victorian notion of "inverts" – which was a way for the Victorians to conceptualise human sexuality. They said that gay men were inverts – i.e. mentally female and that lesbians were also inverts – i.e. mentally male. Yes, that doesn't quite stack up. There are plenty of very manly gay men and very womanly lesbians.

However, in my resurrection of the concept, "Male Invert" is a Gender Identity that says nothing of one's sexual orientation. To me, a Male Invert may sleep with either men or women (or both) and still nonetheless be a Male Invert!

I think the idea of male people who are feminine and female people who are masculine has great potential, and that we can bring in that old Victorian sexology term to cover those things!

So yes, I have borrowed a term from Victorian sexology!

But I have altered its meaning to refer to Inverts of any sexual orientation. It is a Gender Identity, not a Sexual Orientation.

They also had the idea of "Uranians" but I won't be resurrecting that!

This is my story, in one sentence: I thought my way out of Gender Dysphoria.

I no longer have Gender Dysphoria; I am happy being what I am but without identifying as a manly man – because I am not a manly man!

When I see a woman at a table in a café or in a bus I see something of myself in them, I no longer look at them and think "I wish I could have that kind of body" or "I wish I could look like her, my life would be so much better" – my brain now identifies with them in such a way that I don't feel Gender Dysphoria as I once did

When I see them I see myself as I am but in such a way that I don't want to be the same sex as them. When I see women in public I identify with their femininity, and don't dwell on the sex differences. If that makes any sense?

I took care of the problem in my own way, and I believe others may be able to do the same too – sure, not everyone.

But maybe at least some people!

I know that my way is not for everyone, just like the Transgender route was not an option for me.

But I will go into all that later

I will now go over my own personal history of sex and gender

To give you a sense as to where I am coming from!

If you understand my past, you will better understand me and therefore better understand what I'm explaining and what I'm advocating for in this book

We're all different and this is my story:

This is where I'm coming from, this is who and what I am

First off: I am male

I was born in Greece in 1983, my mother is English, and my father is Greek

I look Greek

I was bilingual in English and Greek until I was about three or four, when I left Greece to live in England and stopped speaking Greek, which caused me to stop being able to use or understand it

I wish I could still speak it, it would be really cool to be bilingual

If I had two languages I could have joined the Foreign Office and become a diplomat!

Oh well!

One day, when I was at primary school the teachers hired an entertainer to entertain all the pupils as some kind of treat

We gathered in the hall, the entire school and all the teachers in one room

His act was awful

What he did was, he actually singled me out, from all the other kids and asked me if I was a boy or a girl!!!

He pointed me out and asked me "are you a boy or a girl?"

How awful was that!!!

As though you do that to someone!

What a bastard

One day, at another primary school (which I moved to when we moved house) my class was divided into boys and girls for some extra-curricular activities

The boys went out into the yard to play football and learn football techniques

And the girls went into the school hall to practice acrobatics and the rudiments of ballet

I was excused from football and just sat on my own in the hall whilst all the girls did ballet stuff

I was totally excluded from those two gender-defined groups of children

They laid nothing on for me to do!

I was placed in a category of my own, not in either of the gender groups

Neither the boys nor the girls

And also, why shouldn't have the boys been free to do ballet and the girls free to do football????

Was it 1890 or something???? – this would have been in 1992 or 1993 so perhaps they should have known better....?

And I'm pretty certain most of the girls who did ballet and acrobatics would have been better at football than me!

When I was about that age I tried to feign an interest in football so as to fit in better with the other boys

Even though football did not at all interest me

I was rubbish at it, less than useless

Having me on your team would be worse than being a man down

Zero interest, zero aptitude

I don't get how people can get so passionate about club football although I do find international football less boring as the nation's ego is at stake!

I must admit that I do enjoy a bit of tribalism, but not if it's toxic or stupid…

They always put me in goals as I was so useless on the pitch

Which I think is insulting to goalkeepers

My current name is Edward Penny

But I go by Ed

It used to be Andreas Edward Varcas

Penny is my mother's maiden name

Dreary and Anglo-Saxon

Varcas is Greek for boat

Apparently, my Greek ancestors were sponge-divers, who would have used a boat to go out into the sea and retrieve sponges from the ocean floor

Hence the name "Boat"

Apparently I come from a long line of people who have superior lung capacity, for being able to hold their breath under water.

For a while, I used to think this made me super-efficient at smoking cannabis! – but I don't think it did…

When I went to secondary school I was horribly bullied

I had extravagant hair, a foreign name, and didn't have a Yorkshire accent so on the basis of that I was deemed by some to be unworthy of dignity and life

They mocked me and called me Andrea instead of Andreas

But those fools didn't know that "Andreas" actually means "manly", or "masculine" so the joke was really on them

When I was at (another) secondary school there was a girl named Joanne

There was a long weekend coming up, we were to get the Monday off as some kind of bank holiday

This was at some time in the Spring or Summer

I really cannot remember the details

She gave me her number, and I promised to ring her

I was going to, but me and my mother started making pizzas, so I did that instead of ringing her

Those pizzas were awesome; we made our own dough and grated our own cheese, I will never forget the pizzas me and my mother used to make for as long as I live, they are an abiding memory of my youth

Those pizzas were ace

Anyway, she rang me up in the evening sobbing about the fact I hadn't rung her

Maybe I should have but I have no regrets

Why is this anecdote relevant? Well, it shoes that I preferred making and eating pizzas to the (sexualised) company of females, and I still do, very much so!

But I do enjoy hanging out with females as friends

I eventually ended up going to Warwick University where I studied Sociology

I love Sociology, I think everyone should study it

(I'm cutting out one hell of a lot here!)

Warwick University isn't in Warwick, it's in Coventry, but Warwick sounds more ancient as there is an old medieval castle in the town of Warwick

If the university was as old as the castle then it would be older than Oxford and Cambridge

Warwick University was only founded in 1964, but it sounds much older than it is thanks to people associating it with Warwick castle

It was built after the war to increase the higher education system's capacity, so as to accommodate the post-war baby boom and the extension of higher education to more people, it is in the same generation as York University and Keele University – places like that

I didn't graduate from Warwick though; I had to drop out for various reasons – my degree is from The Open University. I still own a Warwick hoodie, but it is currently way too small for me but it's still there on my clothing rail, in my bedroom. Waiting for me to lose weight and be able to wear it again!

(I am cutting a LOT of my life out here; I'm just sticking to the theme of gender and sex)

When I was there, I lived on one of the corridors in Rootes Residences, I lived in room F48 in F-Block, on the second floor

There was a lad who lived there who was quite a character

He was very confident, outgoing, and charismatic and I liked him

I recently looked him up on the internet and he now has a PhD and is a senior lecturer at a university so well done him

He exercised his dominance and charismatic authority over the corridor by giving people nicknames he had devised

He said that I should be called Eddi. Not Eddy. Not Eddie. But Eddi. That specific spelling. Which is rather feminine. Indeed, it is outright unisex

If you go to Wikipedia and type in "Eddi" you will get a list of people, some of whom are male and some of whom are female. It is a unisex name.

There was a thing this person used to say. He'd say things like "OK lads… and Eddi…" as though I wasn't a lad but was with the lads

However, at this time I called myself Ed. And still do, to this day

But the name stuck even though I wasn't too keen on it although I wasn't opposed to it or anything like that

There are worse things to be called…

In my second year at university, I ended up living in student accommodation in Coventry. I did not like it there. I felt isolated there and on the edge of the civilized world and one or two factors there were to help drive me mad

I had some long-running banter with one of the people there and one of the jokes was that I was called "Proactive Penny the Man Who Does"

Penny is of course a girl's name, short for Penelope. As well as an Anglo-Saxon surname.

There used to be a children's TV show called *Penny Crayon* about a schoolgirl whose drawings magically come to life! It has a catchy tune as you will see if you go and look it up on YouTube

Long story short: I eventually got myself confined to a psychiatric ward. I basically shut myself up in my study bedroom with cannabis and music and did some mad and very deep thinking that literally drove me mad.

The aim was to make me more enlightened and socially skilled and successful. For the details of this period of my life check out my other book, *Feeling Voices*.

I won't go over much of that chapter in my life here

Before I embarked on that course of action, I decided that I wanted to understand how the human mind works. I thought that if I could do this then I could make more friends, find some love interest, and maybe even become a high-powered politician and a leader of men. Which is what I wanted to be able to do.

I used to want to be a politician, but I now have zero interest in that, not anymore. Which is good, as nobody would vote for me!!!

However, at this time, I felt that I had almost zero social skills and was a very socially avoidant.

When I was at college (before I went to Warwick) I would wait out in a nearby park between classes, as opposed to socializing with the other students there. I was scared to make friends or to even venture into the common room.

I made zero friends there, literally zero

And only went into the common room once, on my first day there!

But by the time I was at Warwick this avoidant phase had diminished by quite a bit, and I did make some friends but was still painfully shy at times and missed out on a lot because of this

All my friends were the people I lived with, I was too scared and shy to befriend anyone on my course or join any of the societies, and was way too fat and unfit to have a go joining any of the sporing societies

When trying to figure out how the human mind works, I started off working under the assumption that all minds work more or less alike but after a while I abandoned that and came up with a typology of intellects and psyches.

I basically locked myself up in my study-bedroom with weed and music and made myself insane trying to work things out.

I think I practiced a form of automatic writing, I would just open my mind and pour my thoughts out onto paper, whilst stoned out of my mind and listening to music

Which is actually a good way to spend an afternoon, if you don't do it too often. Getting blasted on weed, putting some music on and brain-storming ideas is fun if you don't do it too often and don't take what you come up with too seriously

I identified two competing faculties of the mind. I called these Intuition and Reason. Reason was how knowledge was produced from direct experience via the senses and Intuition was how knowledge was produced by the imagination using pre-existing knowledge.

I believed that Intuition lived in the left hemisphere of the brain and Reason in the right. I believed that Intuition and Reason competed against each other and would seek to cancel each other out.

I saw them as opposites that worked against each other rather than just different. I created a typology of people. On one end of the scale were people who were entirely Intuitive and on the other people who were entirely governed by Reason. These were I-types and R-types. But there were various intermediary types too. Such as IR types and RI types.

I called I-Types "Dyslexics" because when I was a child I was diagnosed as having dyslexia. I believed that "Dyslexics" used language and words differently to non-Dyslexics and could run rings around them easily and kind of mind-control them

I believed that you could instantly and decisively tell if a person was governed by Reason or Intuition by looking into their eyes!

I remembered some idea floating around at a Dyslexia support group me and my mother went to when I was about ten about Dyslexia having something to do with the left hemisphere of the brain, I looked back and remembered that so dug up the whole Dyslexia thing that was in my past

I couldn't read or write until I was ten, had to have private lessons, without those this book would not exist

Anyway: I literally abandoned reason!

This is the point:

I considered I-types to be superior to R-types. **In Western society, "intuition" is often associated with women and described as mysterious, while "reason" is traditionally linked to men and viewed as masculine, virile, and domineering.**

I abhorred Reason and thought that Intuition was the superior way to go!

At about this time I remember writing that I had been "mis-socialized", but I didn't explore this as I was off my head on weed, perhaps I should have gone down that avenue a bit more?

As I grew madder and madder, I became obsessed with what I called Interest and Identity.

But I didn't think of these in terms of sociological concepts about what is good for you and what you identify as being. Or even as dimensions of one's sexuality or gender identity.

Instead, I saw them as bewildering semiotic energies that governed "human sociability" as I called it. For instance, I believed it was possible to control a person's thoughts and manipulate their attention by altering the physical semiotic environment of a room by the arrangement of objects within a room.

It was like a mad system of Feng Shui

But looking back, these terms can be applied to gender. One can be **interested** in people who are of certain genders and one can **identify** as being of a gender. But at the time I did not make this connection.

And looking back, I think I got my own gender identity and gender interests a bit mixed up

During this phase my mental health degraded rapidly, and I ended up plotting to over-throw the British government via a mass social movement, but that's another story….

I made a lot of noise about this, and I think it is entirely likely that I now have an MI5 file, as a potential subversive although right now I imagine they don't consider me as any sort of threat

They probably just concluded that I was mad and that nobody would ever go along with me! – case closed.

I've read that one in 160 people have an MI5 file and I've read that they have a traffic light system as to how active a person's file is, ranging from green to red via amber

They get lots of criticism when they fail to stop something awful happening on British soil but very little recognition for all the times they get things right. But then earning recognition is not their job…

Whilst I was at Warwick there was a young woman. I thought that I romantically loved her but looking back, I didn't. Instead, I wanted to be her.

I greatly identified with her as opposed to being interested in her. She was feminine, liberated, outgoing, popular, and I thought she was really cool for various reasons.

I wanted to be her so very much, but I thought I loved her and looking back I didn't, at least not romantically

She made the things I found insurmountable seem incredibly easy. Everything worked for her and came naturally to her and all she had to do was be herself. I thought that I had an interest in her, but I didn't, I wanted to be her. I identified with her!

But I didn't realize this until it was too late. It was about Identity rather than Interest!

Anyway, that friendship has been off for over twenty years now (sad face)

When I was eventually locked up in the Coventry psychiatric ward I was once talking to an Occupational Therapist who worked at the hospital. We were having a little chat out in the hospital's little garden, and she gently asked me if I'd ever given any thought to gender.

I told her that I hadn't, and I had not. At least not knowingly!

At some point when I was on the psychiatric ward, I got it into my mind that I was "a woman in a man's body". This blew my mind as I had always considered myself masculine – albeit inadequately masculine.

Maybe it wasn't that I was a rubbish man, maybe I was something other than a man???

I had a very poor record at being a man. I wasn't very good at it. And looking back, I wasn't a man – not as such. I was of course a Male Invert but did not understand this at the time. So therefore I was yet I wasn't!

Being somehow really a woman would somewhat explain why I had so clearly failed as a man. Why I had never had a girlfriend and why I was so unattractive to women. I started to think of myself as being un-self-consciously feminine rather than inadequately masculine.

But it never occurred to me to identify as some kind of woman or as anything other than a common man. And back in 2004 the concept of being "trans" was not a thing so much as it is now. And I drew no connection between being feminine and identifying as a woman. To me the one simply did not follow from the other, and I didn't think doing any of that would change anything anyway. I understood womanhood biologically and didn't buy into notions of social womanhood. But I was aware that that it was an option. So yes, I was open to it. But I chose not to go down that path.

Since my teenage years I believed that I'd have been happier had I been female and if I could have chosen my sex I would have always chosen to be female rather than male. That's just the way I felt. But right now, I am happy being male.

I now know that it is natural to be feminine and male, and that being that way needn't be a source of distress. Not necessarily. I now know that I am neither a man nor a woman – I am a Male Invert, and I am happy with that.

The thing is: I identified **WITH** women but not **AS** a woman even though I thought that mentally and spiritually I was feminine – like how most women are.

I kind of saw myself as being like them in one way but not in others, which was a confused state of mind to be in

I was however happy simply being "a woman in a man's body". That was enough for me, and I saw nothing wrong or disordered about this and no need to change my pro-nouns or to alter my outward appearance accordingly. But even after I'd settled on that as the way to go, I still identified more with women than with men and would have felt better about myself had I had a female body.

But the thing was, to me that was something that was impossible to achieve – like changing my blood group.

Although I had always wanted to be female, for as long as I could remember and always felt more womanly than manly, in terms of personality and psyche. All the worthwhile members of my family were female and if I could have pressed a button to make me female I'd have pressed it. But the thing is, I never did anything about this, I just put it on the back burner and focused on other things, but it was always there, in the background.

My mind is a complex thing, a complex thing to navigate, even for me. But I think that goes for most people, unless they are a bit simple. Literally "simple" as in not complicated, not "simple" as in a bit thick.

I had a lot going on mentally as a young adult, more pressing and demanding than the gender issue, which remained nagging and unresolved, settled in the background

I repressed it a lot rather than addressing it

And this made me into a maladjusted young man.

I've looked up the official psychiatric definition of Gender Dysphoria and I definitely had it, but I was never really aware that I had it, if that makes any sense? Even though I certainly felt that way about things

When I was at Warwick University, I completed the first year of a Sociology degree and on that course, I learnt about personal identities and social identities. A personal identity is how you view yourself and a social identity is how other people identify and treat you. One is about you; the other is social.

The way I saw it my personal identity was "feminine" but that my social identity was "male" as my body was male. I had quite a nuanced take for someone who was so confused and otherwise not all that self-aware.

I made no connection between being feminine "on the inside" and becoming feminine "on the outside". It felt like there was no way out. To me the one did not have to lead to the other. For me it didn't follow. It was enough to simply identify more with femininity than with masculinity.

Also, *I saw no conflict between being a woman in the brain (I will sort of discuss this later) and outwardly identifying as a man and having a male body.* No matter how feminine my psyche may be my fleshy body was most certainly male, and I knew there was nothing I could possibly do about this.

Once I ran that program in my mind, the other programs quieted down and stopped feeding me Gender Dysphoria

And yes, I do very often think of my mind as being like a computer.

For me, declaring myself a woman was a leap that didn't need to be made, and I was aware that doing so would not actually make me into any kind of woman.

And doing so would have made my life much, much more difficult and complicated. It would not be a solution; it would be out of the frying pan and into the fire. It would not have improved my quality of life in anyway – indeed quite the reverse. It would not have been a rational move for me to make.

Thank goodness that at this point in my life no "trans activist" had any influence over me!

When it came to my happiness and wellbeing identifying as feminine and becoming a she/her was a move that did not need to be made!

When I was on the Coventry psychiatric ward there was a trans-woman on Big Brother, the reality TV show. She was called Nadia, and I think she came from Portugal. This was the first time I had ever knowingly seen a trans-woman and she intrigued me.

I felt that I could relate to her a lot, but not entirely. It was nice to see someone who was different out in public just being themselves. I think she actually won that season of Big Brother.

Good on her!

Before being admitted to the hospital, I had a spiritual experience thanks to eating some magic mushrooms!

Back in 2004 these were completely legal in the UK so long as you didn't process them. Which you could do, by either drying them out or freezing them, so as to make them last longer and be able to more easily sell them.

I brought some on the internet from an online "head shop". A head shop is basically a shop that sells drugs paraphernalia such as bongs and rolling papers and "herbal" grinders. Everything but the actual narcotics, basically!

They came to me in the post fresh, in between sheets of tissue paper packed into a little flimsy plastic box. But in the UK magic mushrooms are now a Class A narcotic even if they haven't been processed.

FREE THE SHROOMS!!!!

I was once visiting a stately home in the English countryside where I saw a whole host of magic mushrooms sprouting out of some cow waste

And my sister accidentally stepped on them all!!!

She crushed them under her boots

NOOOOOOOOOOOOOOO!!!!!!

After been under their influence for a couple of hours I was sat on my bed in my study bedroom.

I felt that I was glowing white, that I was unravelling, and I didn't know which way was up!

I had certainly got my money's worth!!

Suddenly a powerful thought suddenly came to me, not in the form of a voice or anything like that, but in the form of an idea, a realization:

It's All About Fitting In!

Thus goes the wisdom of the shrooms

Perhaps I'd been trying to fit into society as a man who was masculine rather than as a man who was not masculine? Feminine even? Or perhaps psychologically androgynous?

I don't know and I have no idea. It's good that I got this revelation though, as at the time I was struggling to learn how I could change to better make friends and influence people, at that time that was my principal concern and yes, it is all about fitting in – or not fitting in!

That is the key to being socially successful

When I was on the Coventry psychiatric ward (detained for 28 days under the 1983 Mental Health Act) a weird and creepy man came in. He was black and had a golden cane, golden teeth, and wore a white glove on one of his hands and was extravagantly dressed.

He played aggressive, shouty music on the CD player that was in the ward's smoking room. It used the "N-word" a lot and mentioned "fucking bitches" (the verb not the adjective) and stuff like that. It had aggressive shouty lyrics that went something like "EAST COAST WEST COAST WE FUCK THEM BITCHES WE FUCK THEM BITCHES HARD I MAKE MY MONEY PIMPING PENIS POWER FOREVER!" and for some reason I found all this intimidating.

The staff made me go into the dormitory I was sleeping in and stay there for about an hour after which this weird creepy man had gone. Never saw him again and thankfully he had taken his repulsive music along with him.

Don't know what happened there! – but I now call that type of music Penis Music.

How could such a person wonder onto a psychiatric ward in the first place, and then get kicked out? Did he just randomly travel to some random psychiatric ward??? And for what reason???

For some reason (when I was on the ward) I got it into my head that I was some kind of "hermaphrodite" as I called it, although the correct term for what I meant is of course "intersex". I took the "I am a woman inside a man's body" way too literally and came to believe that I had feminine bits inside me. There was zero evidence for this and as far as I am aware there is no such condition as that.

And I probably only came to think this because I found it easier to identify as feminine if I was somewhat female – as opposed to identifying as feminine whilst being male.

I hung onto this delusion for a while, but I eventually dismissed it as one of the mad things

I used to think. This was in 2004. You have to remember that at this point public awareness of being trans was nowhere near as high as it is today, in 2025.

How far away 2004 now feels!

I preferred things back then. Especially the internet – before Facebook, Twitter, YouTube. Although the speeds of internet connections back then were terribly slow by today's standards! – young people these days would be shocked and appalled by an old-school 56k modem!

When Nadia came onto Big Brother I had never known of any trans-woman although I was aware that some men wore women's clothes for various reasons.

There was a guy in my hometown who used to go about dressed in female clothes in the 1990s but I have no idea if he identified as a woman or not and I haven't seen him in ages, I wonder who he was and what happened to him… or her…

Fast forward to 2016. I'd stopped taking my anti-psychotic medicine and ended up detained on the Halifax psychiatric ward. I was quite out of my mind and extremely susceptible and sensitive to the thoughts of others. I basically decided that I was feminine. But I never identified as a woman, no matter how hard I thought this. That did not seem like a logical leap to make, even back then and even though I considered myself to be more womanly than manly.

I knew that I could never possibly be a woman as much as I knew not to go into any of the "female only" areas on the ward and that I was a boy rather than a girl. This was back when psychiatric wards were mixed sex. Today most of them aren't. Which I think is best for everyone.

I came to think of myself in terms of having a certain "brain sex". I considered my brain to be female and the rest of my body to be male. I will go into this later.

At the time I thought this was a good mix – the male body is bigger and stronger than a female body and I thought that females were more intelligent and civilized than males! I saw femininity as being cerebral and masculinity to be bodily and physical.

I believed that a female mind and a male body were the perfect combination to receive from

Mother Nature! Women have not contributed to fucking up the world as much as men have.

A female mind was a better thing to have than a male mind and a male body was better thing to have than a female body – so I reasoned. Jackpot!

And having a dick does not automatically make you macho. Far from it!

I believed that was a really cool combination for me to have, and even though I didn't use the word at the time that was more or less when I started thinking of myself as a Male Invert – and of "Male Invert" being a legitimate gender identity!

Although I would not use that term for many years to come…

I was once in one of the activity rooms on the ward feeling really, really crappy. I complained to one of the members of staff, one of the nurses. This nurse casually informed me that this was because it was "your time of the month". Why say that? How would they even know?

Also, for some reason when I was on that ward the nurses put a big plastic bin in my room (which was on one of the male corridors) – the type of bin into which women deposit used sanitary products. Why do that????? I'm a man!!!!

At one point I demanded a pregnancy test, my sanity was that far gone. Also, at this time my dog was having a phantom pregnancy as dogs sometimes do – I thought that perhaps this was happening to me or that the nurses may have induced such a condition by slipping me certain pills without me knowing. I thought that the nurses were giving me hormone pills. There was no basis for this belief, it was entirely psychotic.

I was aware that in World War II the Allies tried to feminize Adolf Hitler by slipping him estrogen pills to make him less aggressive, but I don't think they succeeded

Anyway, by 1944 Hitler was an absolute junkie, he was on all manner of drugs and was quite a wreck, so it wasn't necessary for the allies to slip him pills to make him weaker and less able – and he was under the influence of a socially ambitious quack doctor who gave him all sorts of crap: steroids, opioids, amphetamines, hormones, cocaine – etc.!

By the time he ended up shooting himself he was a total mess, he'd totally lost the plot (if he ever really had it in the first place…)

But I digress.

At the hospital they also took lots and lots of blood samples even though they knew I hated having to have blood extracted from me. I thought they were monitoring my sex hormones or even trying to clone me

Because that's one thing the world really needs… clones of me!!! – Mini-Eds!!!

For the rest of the time on the ward I felt more feminine than masculine. But as I got used to this idea, I stopped feeling that way, the novelty wore off. I just felt that I was me, not a person who is X or Y, or a member of category A or B. And I felt no need to adopt any kind of new identity.

And treating people as individuals, not as members of a group – has always been important to me and something I try and live up to

If I ever fail to remember or live up to that kindly remind me.

When I was on that ward, I was obsessed with gender. When I went onto that ward, I had Gender Dysphoria and when I left it I didn't. I left it behind in the madhouse. I lost it due to thinking about it a lot in an ordered and institutionalized clinical setting.

I've seen some of my notes, and in them it says that I once told one of the nurses that I felt like me being on the ward was like being "a whore in a nunnery"!!!

But I'm not sure what that really means, I was quite far out of my mind

I think I came to see that it doesn't really matter if I was male or female so long as I was authentically myself and this realization took a great weight off my psyche and enabled me to move forwards more, in a better direction

Sex started to seem more like an irrelevant detail to me

So what if I'm male??? I'm still me and always will be, no matter the genitals

I came to see my humanity as being in harmony with itself, not in conflict

Meeting lots of different people helped me a lot too. It was a very intense experience. I did a lot of thinking there. And lots of crazy, convoluted things happened to me on that ward!

I am six-foot two-inches tall, heavily built, and have a big hairy body.

I have broad masculine shoulders and narrow non-child-bearing masculine hips

And a beard – I have a beard as shaving always cuts me up. A total blood bath! – and using a shaving machine doesn't shift my stubble. But I do think beards are cool, so I am not too bothered. Anyway, beards are cool!

I knew that no matter how feminine I was inside I was not at all feminine on the outside – which is basically the Male Invert condition. I could never ever pass as a woman.

For me, wearing women's clothes would only exaggerate and broadcast the fact that I'm a man. People would look at me and see a man in a dress. Not a person who is really a woman but who somehow comes in the shape of a man.

I could never pass as a woman. Being able to do that would be something else, but I can't, which makes being Trans much less of a good option for me. And it's not as if doing so would make me female either. So nope. I won't be doing that. But you do you.

If I go into town wearing jeans and a hoodie nobody would notice me. If I were to go into town wearing a big flowing flowery summer dress I may feel comfortably cool in Summer, but I would stick out massively – and I don't want to be visible in that way, be it wearing masculine clothes or feminine clothes.

For instance, I would never go into town dressed as a high-fantasy wizard, even though I think that would be cool and would like an actual wizard hat. Or wearing Lederhosen. Sure, that would on one level be very cool. But I am not an exhibitionist. And no, I am not saying that males who dress as women are exhibitionists. I do not believe that is what motivates them. But sure, maybe some people who do that do it for attention.

My point is that as a Transwoman I would stand out as a minority much more than being a Male Invert. I am pulled towards being a Male Invert by many factors and am also pushed away from being Trans by other factors. Simply put, I would hate it if I had to be a Transwoman.

As a person who wants happy, content, simple, and easy life, doing that would be entirely counter-productive and would solve nothing – even if it did somehow align my outward appearance with my inner disposition

It would solve nothing and make things way, way worse and wasn't even necessary for me

I know that it is possible to "transition" from one sex to another, but I don't think that doing so actually changes your sex – which is one reason why I didn't go down that path, if there was a magic button that could transform men into women and women into men then that would be entirely different, but no such button exists.

As I became more and more comfortable with the idea of being a Male Invert (even though I did not use the term until very recently) I stopped expecting people to think of me as womanly. I was clearly a man, and I knew there was no way for me to possibly change that

This is where my valued principle of treating others as individuals comes from.

It was up to me to show the world that you can be a man without having masculine personality traits and that you can have feminine traits without presenting to the world as a woman

I realized that I was under no obligation to be a manly man!

And I discovered that one of the meanings of life is to become an individual, on your own terms.

I accepted that I was male and a man and decided that was that whilst hoping people would simply take me for who I was.

Yet I definitely considered my mind to be female. I just felt as though I identified with women more than with men. I did not see this combination as being absurd or abnormal, or a cause for any concern. I could relate much more to femininity than to masculinity. As I said before, I thought that being outwardly male and inwardly female was the best possible deal to have received from Mother Nature.

I don't think distinctions about "inside" or "outside" are valid or make much sense. I think that it is best to have a holistic view of yourself as a unitary entity, rather than seeing yourself as a bundle of faculties and ideas and impressions gathered under one roof

I believed that in a state of nature women would gather berries and fruit, raise children, create tools, make cave paintings, and mix potions and light fires whereas the men would bash each other's heads in with rocks and hunt saber-toothed tigers! I believed that a patriarchal social order only came to be once humans started living in settlements and started to grow crops and live in houses and have organized religion that we in today's age would recognize.

I believed that before settled civilization women were in charge in a matriarchy and that women were best suited to cerebral pursuits and men to physical pursuits. On account of them normally being feminine rather than masculine not on account of them being female rather than male.

But of course, such talk about a "state of nature" can only ever be conjecture. It is entirely speculative. However, I think it can be an interesting thing to think about even if it is only pseudo-anthropology!

It was certainly a common thing to do in the European enlightenment. Particularly when imagining a kind of "original position".

Did I have Gender Dysphoria? Absolutely, yes, although it was over-shadowed by various (other) mental health concerns that were much more pressing. Such as "drug-induced psychosis" and later Schizophrenia, and later still Paranoid Schizophrenia!

They basically updated my diagnosis over the course of many years!

And Gender Dysphoria **is** a mental health concern; it is included in the current version of the Diagnostic and Statistical Manual of Mental Disorders (DSM) which is basically the "bible" of the psychiatric profession that ensures standardized diagnosis and treatment of people with certain conditions between individual doctors and hospitals

I have looked at the criteria and I met enough for them to apply that diagnosis to me. And according to my research if you want to go in for "gender-reassignment" surgery then you need to have been diagnosed as having Gender Dysphoria by two specialist doctors, according to the criteria of the DSM.

However, I did nothing about this. I repressed and ignored it and thankfully I eventually grew out of it without having to change who I was as a person. I have always identified more with women than with men. Most of my family are female.

By becoming a Male Invert I did not have to change anything – not a thing. I always was one, but didn't realize it

I eventually managed to think my way out of my Gender Dysphoria and very much decided against becoming trans, as for me that would have caused way more problems than it would have solved, indeed I didn't think it would actually resolve anything.

It would have made my life objectively worse – not better!

It did not feel like a logical progression for me and would have made my life way more complicated

But if I could have somehow made myself transform into an actual adult female human then I would have done that, if there was a button that could do that, I'd have pressed it.

But there wasn't and there isn't. I eventually came to understand that there was nothing wrong with me. Nothing to be worried about. I eventually came to feel right and authentic, not lacking or disordered.

Feminine men and Masculine women are natural and ordinary – there is no reason for an invert of any sex to become trans. There is nothing wrong with being an invert, it is not a problem that needs solving. It is a legitimate category of human!!!

But sure, if you'd rather go trans then you do you.

Basically, I thought myself out of Gender Dysphoria. My feelings changed. I realized that I was already authentic and that there was nothing wrong with me or that was stopping me from being who I truly was.

I came to see that being male or female – or masculine of feminine – was not of such great importance as I once thought it was

Being an authentic and well-rounded individual started to seem more important to me

I came to accept myself and my feelings of Gender Dysphoria evaporated. And I managed to do this by thinking critically about sex and gender. By acquiring an understanding of sex and gender that was more complex than "men wear trousers and women wear skirts"

And for me, this worked. The problem stopped being a problem. I'd go as far to say that it was solved.

I found my refuge and my sanctuary in the identity of Male Invert. And I have made my home there. And I intend to stay in that place.

Thanks to actually thinking about sex and gender, I came to understood (albeit towards the back of my mind) the difference between gender and sex, between feminine and female – **and that not all feminine people are women and not all women are feminine**

But yes, for a while I considered myself a woman who had a male body. Until I convinced myself that that made zero sense. As I will explain. I really did think my way out of that one!

I felt that I did not fit into the standard definitions. I was definitely unhappy about being a man but saw no way out, until I stopped being bothered by that by running different programs in my psyche, and trying to switch off some of the older ones

If there was a button that would change your sex just by pressing it would I press it?

I'm not sure.

At one time I definitely would have as I wanted a female body, as I considered myself otherwise female and I wanted to be a member of the female sex. I did not adequately distinguish between gender qualities and sex. But I no longer feel that way, I managed to think my way out of Gender Dysphoria. And I'm sure others could too.

However, the thing is in our society men have a superior social status to women, even today. And I think I could better help change that as man, as opposed to as a woman.

Also, women are also more physically vulnerable than men. And can get pregnant, which is something I would not want to happen to me. Also, I am now genuinely happy with the way I am, and I like that. And for all I know I may not like being a woman! I wouldn't want to menstruate, that's for sure. I do not envy having to go through that every month. So, right now I'm thinking that I would no longer press it.

Although I definitely would have in the past, without any hesitation.

But my final answer to this conundrum is going to have to be "I don't know". I'd have to give it more thought. Although I feel no strong desire to transform into a woman. I have been male for 42 years now and am now settled into my horrible body

But the thing is: I am now happy as a Male Invert. I don't know how happy I'd be as a woman. For I know being a woman is horrible. So I'd probably stick to what I am sure makes me happy. I think that is the most rational course of action.

Anyway… I currently have other things to worry about

For me, all that stuff is now mostly in my past

So…..

That's the story of me and sex and gender!

<u>I will now explain my own personal take on Sex and Gender!</u>

Sure, this may be different to whatever paradigm you operate but I think my way makes sense!

Sex

Either you are born with a body that can carry a baby, or you are built with a body that is meant to be able to make a person who can carry a baby pregnant

You are either built to be a mother or to be a father

You either produce sperm in your testicles or carry eggs about in your ovaries

If you are supposed to produce sperm, then you are of the male sex and if you carry eggs inside you then you are of the female sex

A male human is called a "man" and a female human a "woman" – that is how Biological Sex works. That's what it is. **That's all it is.**

I don't think there is much you can do to change this

Just like your blood group

Although yes, you can have cosmetic procedures done on your body so as to make it resemble that of someone of the opposite sex *and if that works for you then all power to you, that's good!*

But there's no way I would ever have that done to my body and it wouldn't even be a vagina; my understanding is that it would be a kind of penis tucked in on itself – I don't want one of those!

And they *are* opposites; you can either be one or the other (not counting those with intersex conditions but apparently those people tend to choose one sex to be classified as)

Being both male and female is not really possible, but yes, being both masculine and feminine is – that is what non-binary people are. Kind of both in one sense, and neither in another. I think that's really cool but I personally prefer being a Male Invert

One's sex is genetically determined, to use a cliché that I don't much care for "it is in your DNA"

In that regard it is like eye colour, skin pigmentation, blood group, and what your hair is like, or how tall you are – etc.

It is based on which sex chromosomes you inherit from your parents

However, one's sex alone says nothing as to what you are like as a person, but it does determine where you start from, on life's journey

Humanity is naturally divided into two biological categories: male and female

Socially, this translates as there being two (main) social categories: masculine and feminine

Traditionally male people have to act masculine and female people feminine, but not so much these days – at least not in the West

Sex is biological. It is about WHAT you are rather than WHO you are. It is not really personal; it is more social. It is about what your place is in society, how you fit into things.

It needn't say anything about you any more than being 6 foot 2 high makes you anything other than tall

And that's how tall I am

And male bodies are noticeably different to female bodies, for instance bone density, skull shape, metabolism – that sort of thing

It's not just about genitals; those are just the cherry on the cake! The most obvious way of telling!

Some people who think that sex counts for nothing and that it's all about gender identity say that focusing on peoples' genitals (i.e. their sex) is weird, and make a lot of noise about that idea, calling it creepy and pervy

They say that it's creepy and make fun of it – "those people who are obsessed with the genitals of others!"

But this is cheap and easy and doesn't hold up, it's rhetoric not reason

And truth be told**, one's sex carries enormous societal significance that goes beyond the genitals**, the genitals are only a sign of what sex you are, they don't determine what sex you are, it's not as if the only difference between a male and female body is the genitals

But don't let the truth get in the way of a good rhetorical device!

Or at least something that to some passes as a good rhetorical device…

Also: it is a fact that **a penis can be used as a weapon**, in sexual violence such as rape. Certain activists seem to totally ignore that, possibly because they themselves have never suffered from sexual violence and are too caught up with themselves to think of others? – that's one reason why we segregate changing rooms according to sex. The safety factor, and the weirdness factor.

Socially, people of one sex getting naked together is totally different to people of opposite sexes getting naked together. It is totally different, no matter what some say. To disregard this is to ignore how our society actually works. In our society the sexual segregation of certain types of place is a part of our culture. That's how society works. But I will go into all that later.

And there is a word for wilfully violating the rules and conventions that govern how we behave towards others: "anti-social".

I don't think some people really realise this, that they haven't really thought things through. Or outright don't give a shit about people other than themselves. One of the two.

A person's genitals are a part of WHAT they are – they don't define what you are. They are only an accompanying sign. A reliable accompanying sign. Having a penis is a very reliable indicator of who is or is not a man. Men are supposed to use the male changing rooms because they are men, not because they have a penis. That's the basis on which sexual segregation works. *It is sexual segregation, not genital segregation.*

So I think that objection is a bit stupid, to be honest

It is cheap and easy – flippant and facile. A substitute for saying something helpful or intelligent.

I was once in an online community and saw a liberal atheist MAN who seems to think he is God lecturing a WOMAN who had suffered sexual abuse in the past about how she should welcome people with penises into her changing rooms, and she was having none of that, and good on her.

He was talking down to her and obviously didn't care about how she felt. He was actually trying to correct the way she felt and was lecturing her, as though she was in the wrong and her wicked and immoral behaviour and attitudes needed correcting.

I'd actually call that type of dismissive attitude misogyny

I always favour the underdog, that's my nature, and females and transwomen are both underdog categories in their own way, and my instinct is to support both of them, even when demands conflict. But as a Male Invert that is not my conflict, as I will explain later.

Anyway, I think changing rooms are barbaric. I think that at swimming pools and gyms they should have changing cubicles. Far more civilized.

Anyway, I hate gyms and swimming pools. I abhor physical activity.

Sex Presentation (Sex Identity)

The next factor is what I call **Sex Presentation – or Sex Identity**

That is what sex you identify as being and present to the world as a member of:

Male or Female

Regardless of your actual sex

This can also be called "Social Sex" – as opposed to "Biological Sex"

It is about your societal self-identification, not your biological status as either male or female

Basically, to choose a sex presentation is to choose a social identity for yourself

What sex you are born as determine your options as to what you can become

It can be stated in two ways:

Sex Identity = *Biological Sex + Social Sex*
Sex Identity = *Sex + Sex Presentation*

For instance:

- *Male Sex + Female Sex Presentation =* ***Transwoman***
- *Male Sex + Male Sex Presentation =* ***Man***
- *Female Sex + Female Sex Presentation =* ***Woman***

- *Female Sex + Male Sex Presentation = **Transman***

Transwoman, Man, Woman, and Transman are all different Sex Identities

Male Inverts are **Men** and Female Inverts are **Women**. Those are *Sex Identities*.

"Male Invert" and "Female Invert" *are gender identities*.

Having re-assignment surgery and "transitioning" is a Sex Presentation issue in that it changes what sex you present to the world as being and indicates how you want to be treated and how you want to fit into society – but it does not actually change your Sex. But yes, it changes what sex you look like, which I suppose counts for something?

Were a man to use my terminology and say, "my sex presentation is female" they are basically saying "treat me as a woman". It doesn't make them a woman *biologically*, but it means they want to be a woman *socially* – **and it is entirely possible for one to change one's social sex. But not so much one's biological sex.**

And a person can be biologically a man and socially a woman. That's what Transwomen are!

Should changing your Sex Presentation change your bathroom and changing room credentials? – I think it depends. I will explain this later on in this book.

Absolutely none at all

Can A Woman Have A Penis?

Depends on what you mean by woman!

You cannot be **biologically** a woman and have a penis, no

By definition a woman is a person with a vagina, the actual word "woman" comes from "womb man" – so a female person can't have a penis. If you have a penis, you are not female

However, "woman" **is also a social category**

I'd say that a person with a penis can never be a woman in the biological sense, but may be one in the social sense – by adopting feminine pronouns and **presenting** as a woman

I wouldn't call a man who presents as a woman a "woman" but I would call them a "lady"

So, to use the old slogan "transwomen are women" – no, they aren't.

But they are Ladies

They should be treated as ladies, but not as women

How exactly is up to **The Community of Women** *and not for me (a man) to say* – but we will explore that later

Unless they are a transman, all people who are biologically female – women – are also socially female – ladies. But membership of The Community of Women comes from ones sex, the sex one was born as. It is a community of Sex, not of Gender.

And with transmen, transmen aren't men. But they are blokes

I've seen men being called "penis-havers" and I don't much like this

I see nothing wrong about being a Lady or a Bloke: a feminine man or a masculine woman who wants to be treated as though they are of the opposite sex

But of course, one can be non-binary. There are a great many was available in which to be human and being able to choose what type of human you are is a basic right, although some things are not subject to change.

A man cannot become a Woman, but they can become a Lady. And a woman cannot become a man, but they can become a Bloke

I think all this is fair and reasonable.

Genders

These are personal characteristics that are associated with people of each sex

And these vary between both culture and epoch

And in any society there are competing masculinities and femininities

For instance, in an American high-school dramas there are "nerds" and "jocks" – two different ways of being male, two different masculinities – each as masculine as the other! – one set loves competitive, contact sports. And the other Star Trek and Dungeons and Dragons. Both are different ways of being male.

But yes, there are dominant codes and alternative codes. For instance "gay man" is not the dominant way of being male, but it is now an accepted way of being male

In Stanley Kubrick's film *Full Metal Jacket* a bunch of young conscripts are moulded into a certain kind of man – a US Marine. With the aim of them being shipped over to Vietnam to fight in the war there. This film portrays the way in which young males are turned into a certain type of man. Through being broken down and then rebuilt. Ultimately, this amounts to dehumanisation. They are stripped of their humanity and turned into killing machines, but the thing is, Vietnam veterans suffer from a lot of PTSD, which would indicate that they were not successfully turned into killing machines.

There is Masculine and Feminine – but these are not the same as Male and Female

"Masculine" traits are traits traditionally associated with men

"Feminine" traits are those traditionally associated with women

I think thinking about it all like this is better than making one list of "masculine traits" and another beside it of "feminine traits" and then comparing the two

What is considered Masculine is based on what men are expected to be like in society, and being Feminine is based on what women are expected to be like in society

And they are not just descriptive: they are prescriptive. They are roles. Which people grow up to inhabit – and if you don't live up to them you can get into trouble

And people do enforce certain codes onto others – the anti-trans stuff is a traditionalist reaction against the liberalisation of society's gender system. The reality of trans people threatens that system and inspires vigilante gender policing – both against trans people and against those who may even consider it

As a Male Invert I'm all for modernising society's traditional sex and gender system

Here's the thing:

- Not all men are Masculine, and not all masculine people are men
- Not all women are Feminine, and not all feminine people are women

They don't come hand in hand and being (for instance) Masculine does not make you in any way Male, unless you also happen to be Male

And also, let's not forget the non-binary option!

There are many ways of being Masculine and many ways of being Feminine

Being a transwoman is one way of being Feminine (femininity for men) and being a transman (masculinity for women) is one way of being Masculine!

Yet on the other hand, Transwoman can be thought of as a form of masculinity as it is a thing males do, and Transman can be thought of as a form of femininity as it is a thing females do.

You can argue it either way. If we consider Male Inverts then yes, that is a masculinity as it is a way of being male. But it is also a way of being feminine, i.e. a femininity!

I think this shows us how sex and gender are complicated and not at all clear-cut!

The thing is though, there can be a lot of gender policing and oppression in societies, for instance in Iran you cannot be a gay man, they will hang you if you so much as even think a gay thought

And although not illegal, if I were to venture out onto the mean streets of central Halifax on a Friday or Saturday night wearing a flowing flowery summer dress and high-heels I would get the shit beaten out of me. So that's one example of gender policing doing by vigilante action, rather than the state.

That shouldn't be, but it is.

Spirits And Brain Sex

In Version 1.0 of this book I said that there is such a thing as Masculine and Feminine souls, or spirits, or whatever

I don't really buy that now though, even though I believe all humans have an eternal soul, which is the basis for things such as consciousness and agency/free will

Sounds a bit un-scientific – new age even?

However, I think that Masculinity and Femininity may have a neurological basis, in the brain

Here's the question: is masculinity and femininity the product of "brain sex"?

Or is it some kind of spiritual way of being? An ineffable essence?

I don't know what the basis is, but I think masculinity and femininity are both very real

Maybe they are just different categories in which to sort individual humans? And that "masculine" and "feminine" are just the words we use to refer to certain clusters of personal qualities – as opposed to actual concrete categories????

But that doesn't mean we need to go on and on about Brain Sex, it doesn't matter why or how one is either Masculine or Feminine, it doesn't matter

Just take people as individuals, that's what I say

And of course, it is possible to be neither a Masculine human or a Feminine human, you can always be non-binary!

Heterosocial and Homosocial

Sam Peckinpah's 1977 war film *Iron Cross* tells the story of a platoon of German soldiers on the Eastern Front in World War II, on the run in 1943 after Germany's defeat at the battle of Kursk – a big turning point in the war in the East

In this film there is a horrible and obnoxious officer called Stransky who is desperate to win the Iron Cross for all the prestige and status it brings as he if from an aristocratic family with a long tradition of military service. He even requested a transfer to the Eastern front from the relative safety of occupied France, so hungry was he for the Iron Cross – a highly thought of award for bravery in action.

Adolf Hitler himself had won it in the Frist World War. It came in First Class and Second Class. Hitler won the First Class. Having it basically made you an instant hero in Nazi Germany.

But Stransky doesn't seek to be awarded it honestly. Instead, he blackmails a subordinate officer named Triebig into recommending him for the Iron Cross for fighting off a Soviet attack – even though during the Soviet attack Stransky was cowering in his bunker, away from the action and out of harm's way. Indeed the defense was actually led by Triebig.

In the privacy of a bunker, Stransky asks Triebig whether he prefers the company of men or the company of women. To entrap him in such a way that no matter how he'd answer Stransky could say he was gay! Which was of course punishable by death, in the German army of 1943, under the Nazis.

If he said he preferred the company of men, then that would mean he was gay and erotically loved men (like something out of ancient Greece!) and if he said that he preferred the company of women then that would make him an effeminate sissy who is most likely gay and wants to sit with old ladies, knitting and sipping tea. There would be no possible answer for him to give without opening him up to being accused of being gay. A hanging offence.

There is such a thing as being Heterosocial or Homosocial. Heterosocial people prefer the company of the other sex and Homosocial people prefer the company of the same sex.

Most people engage in both homosocial and heterosocial relations.

Personally, I enjoy the company of both, I suppose that I am Bisocial. This has nothing at all to do with my sexual preferences. I have known some people who are Heterosocial and others who are Homosocial although I think most people are Bisocial.

This is something we need to be aware of if we want to be able to understand the realities of Sex and Gender

It is a factor when coming to understand others as individuals, which is something we must strive to do, it is a means of understanding others

Anyway, (Spoiler Alert!!) in the end Stransky gets shot dead by little Russian kid with a tommy gun who he can't shoot as he has no idea how to reload his gun, which is good because he was an arsehole…

Androphilia and Gynephilia

I have been considering abandoning the concepts "homosexual" and "heterosexual". I don't like them, and they feel very limiting to me.

And those terms each come with so much baggage attached to them, in the form of stereotypes. It also sounds very heteronormative to me, and I don't much like that. I do not believe that such labels reflect the reality of real people.

Also, being Gay is different to being Homosexual. Being Gay is a way of being Homosexual, but one can have a Homosexual disposition without leading a Gay life. And I think the same goes for Lesbians.

An Androphile is any person who is attracted to men and a Gynephile is any person who is attracted to women. Regardless of what their own sex is. And it is possible to be both an Androphile and a Gynephile. Or bisexual, in traditional terms.

I think that Androphilia vs. Gynephilia is a good alternative to the Homosexual vs. Heterosexual dichotomy because it is less restraining, less prescriptive. And it is easier to be both Androphilic and Gynephilic than to be both Homosexual and Heterosexual.

It makes sexual orientation a matter of attraction, not a matter of what you actually do. Both are important. Perhaps we could operate the distinction between Homosexual and Heterosexual alongside the distinction between Androphile and Gynephile?

And I think people should consider adopting it. I think doing so would make being Gay or Lesbian less of a big deal, I think it is more personal than "homosexual" or "heterosexual". That's what I think anyway!

That way, gay men and straight women could be in one category, and straight men and lesbians could be in another. Perhaps that would work? I have no idea.

It makes sexual orientation a question of taste and attraction, rather than of personal identity or lifestyle – a matter of inner disposition rather than outward behavior

It is more personal and less social

Think Of The Children!

Most parents are good people who love their children unconditionally and want whatever's best and right for them

However, I think that the good intentions of parents can be hijacked by people with an ideological axe to grind, but who appear to be helpful and concerned

Such people prey on the natural concerns parents have for the welfare of their children and try to force things onto peoples' children for their own reasons, things that needn't be forced on to children and that don't naturally follow or make sense

Imagine, someone has a little boy. Let's call him Gerald. Gerald does not like playing with toy cars, he prefers dolls. And Gerald does not care for football or playing rough games with the boys in the playground, at school. Instead, he fits more easily in with the girls. And behaves and conducts himself more like a girl. He is gentle, quiet, sensitive, introspective.

This may lead to a good and loving parent to think "Gerald is not a boy; Gerald is REALLY a girl – therefore Gerald is trans!" – and then raise him under that assumption, as though that is somehow true and valid

This does not follow. Being FEMININE does not make you in any way "truly" FEMALE.

To be "truly" female you need XX Chromosomes, that's all

No XX Chromosomes = not female

Regardless of how you behave or what you are like as a female

Gerald is not "really" a girl "trapped" in a male body. None of that makes any sense, even if you only think about it for five or six seconds

And being male is not caused by being masculine, it is caused by being male – so being feminine would not make a person not male and somehow "truly" female

A feminine boy is not a girl and is no less male than a masculine boy, who loves football, tanks, and watching Formula 1

A feminine boy is in no way female, he is still male regardless of any feminine traits he may have or behaviours he may exhibit

He should therefore be treated as a boy – **until he himself, as an adult, under his own free will** (and without any influence from his parents or other people) can decide otherwise

Dressing him up so that his sex presentation is "female" just because he is feminine rather than masculine makes zero sense – it doesn't follow

And anyway, male person cannot be "truly" female – it really is a matter of either/or

Either you are male or you're female, there needn't be anything confusing about this

The whole messing with the sex presentation of children thing assumes that a male cannot be feminine and a female cannot be masculine – **they medicalise inversion and make it something to be cured, or treated**

As a Male Invert I find this outrageous

Gerald is not Geraldine

Gerald is a HETEROSOCIAL boy who is feminine.

Maybe when he is older he could decide to become Geraldine, or embrace being a Male Invert?

But as he is, he's just a kid. Just let him be himself, without imposing stuff on him either way.

He is in no way female, hence making him present as being female does not need to be done. It does not follow. And as a child he is incapable of making that decision – and that decision can only come from an informed adult

It's like "yesterday the sun was shining outside, therefore for the rest of my life when I wake up in the morning I will always get out of the left side of my bed" – it's really down at that low level of not making sense

Gerald is not an informed adult, and it would be wrong to make that decision for him. He is not a man or a woman. He is a child.

There isn't even a problem with him being feminine, that's only an issue to people who are obsessed with sex and gender – and have some weird axe to grind

People who say that Gerald is really in fact a girl are basically say that it is impossible for a male person to be feminine! – they deny that the category of Male Invert exists

Gerald is not a girl. Gerald has XY chromosomes and a penis and testicles. There are absolutely no grounds for confusion as to whether he is a boy or a girl. And whatever gendered traits he may have, or behaviours he may exhibit have zero bearing on his sex

A change in his Sex Identity can only come from Gerald himself, once he is grown up. It is wrong to feed him ideas and put thoughts in his mind or confuse him.

We should treat boys and girls as boys and girls – not as men and women.

Children can be very sensitive and pick up on things very easily. And it may seem like things are coming from them when in reality they have picked up on them form other people. When I was a kid I would parrot my mother's opinions about various things.

Choosing a gender identity requires sexual maturity as does having a sexuality. There is no such thing as a homosexual or a heterosexual five-year-old. Children are asexual until sexual maturity kicks in and their brains become more developed.

If Gerald were to ask his parents whether he is a boy or a girl the only responsible thing for them to do would be to say: "you have a penis therefore you're a boy. But that doesn't matter one bit, it does not define who you are as a person. You go ahead and you do you. I will always love and support you no matter what"

His parents should be supportive and loving and not care about what gender he most aligns with. It shouldn't matter. Just let him sort himself out, and make sure he knows he will always be supported and loved no matter what choices he makes once he comes of age.

There is no need for Gerald to feel any confusion and his parents should guide him towards clarity.

I think that children should be educated about gender and sex in the way that they are about human reproduction – about "the birds and the bees" but not in ways that lead them towards any one conclusion. And this ought to be done without making a big deal of it all. Children should focus on being boys and girls, not men or women.

If under his own free will and without any external influence he were to decide that he wants to live as a girl then that would be different. But if that were to happen his parents should educate him some more and help him better understand what's going on, and help him sort himself out rather than encouraging him or discouraging him from doing whatever

As a Male Invert I find it offensive that people like me are very often guided and manipulated into going down the Trans route as though that is the only option and being a Male Invert is not possible, is equated with languishing in some sorry state that you need saving from

Feminine Males are treated with hormones and given surgery without the possibility of being a Male Invert being made clear to them. This should not be the case.

And a lot of people who pretend to help concerned parents with Invert children have a political, ideological motivation. An axe to grind. Not all but some. They don't see individuals, they see categories. They are not out to help and inform, they have a political agenda to push.

Trans-radicals seem to be obsessed with sex and gender. They basically deny that a male person can be feminine – they think that if a male person is feminine then that somehow invalidates the fact they are male and (in some magical and undefined way) means they are somehow "truly" female, even if they have zero female anatomy and have XY chromosomes.

It just doesn't make sense!

This is what it is: It's Invert-phobia

It denies that "Invert" (either male or female) is a valid identity, a valid way of being human

It is wrong to force masculinity on boys, and it is wrong to force femininity on them. **Those things are for adults**, and they should be introduced to them as teenagers.

Just let them be kids and enable them to grow up understanding the realities of sex and gender, beyond "girls wear pink and play with dolls" and "boys wear blue and play with toy cars" – who says those things are true! Clearly some boys do prefer dolls and some girls toy cars! – *both the traditional gender paradigm and the more modern liberal gender paradigm clearly has problems with this reality.*

It really should not be much of an issue.

Certain trans-activists literally treat being an invert with surgery and other medical interventions – **they literally medicalise being an Invert**, they see it as a thing to be corrected. As an Invert myself, I very much disapprove of this.

It is as though they see being an Invert as an illness, a condition that needs correcting. Sometimes by hormonal treatments.

Truly, proponents of both the traditional paradigm and the liberal paradigm are obsessed with sex and gender and obsessed with enforcing gender norms, but in different ways

"You aren't living up to society's expectations as to how a male lives and what a male is like… therefore you're not really male, here have some hormones!!" is just as bad (if not worse than) "Don't play with those Barbies! You're a boy so play with these toy cars instead!"

Both of these are bonkers, really – in their own way

It's madness. Born out of an ideological motivation to push their personal gender ideologies. Be it the traditional one, or what I call the "liberal" paradigm. And if you look at their personal gender ideologies, they most likely won't make much sense, as they ignore the realities of sex and gender

Don't listen to the activists. Or whatever you want to call them, whatever guise they come in. A male can be feminine without being female and a female can be masculine without being male. There is nothing wrong with that. Trans activists deny this and push surgery, hormones, and a change in sex presentation on little children, by charming and conning their loving parents.

The humane and loving option is to support your kids no matter what and to inform them to help them make an intelligent decision and to better understand themselves.

The medicalisation of inversion is despicable, really. It's manipulation and abuse. I find all this personally offensive, as a Male Invert. I feel as though those people are against my right to be exist as a Male Invert because they see male invertness to be a problem that needs curing, or a solution – sometimes with surgery.

They actually deny that a male can possess feminine qualities. If you are a male and have feminine qualities then to them you aren't really male, and you need your genitals re-arranging. No thanks!

Children can be very sensitive and may pick up from their parents the ideas that they got from trans-activist sources. They believe in Santa Claus. They cannot decide things for themselves like adults can. And it is wrong to make certain decisions **FOR** them.

Nobody has the right to decide the gender identity for any child, which is what actually happens when a parent decides "my child must be trans!", or "my boy is really a girl!!!"

Just let the kids be kids, let them develop on their own, don't force things onto them, be they traditional gender roles or more "alternative" gender roles.

And yes, this has to be said: I think *some* parents really want their children to be recognised and acknowledged as being in some way "special" and that deciding that their five-year-old boy is really a girl can satisfy that. I'm pretty sure that happens.

Especially with pushy middle-class types who are intelligent enough to be able to look things up on the internet.

He is otherwise unremarkable but "My darling little Timmy is really a girl, don't you know!"

If Gerald wants to play with Barbies then let him do that and if he wants to paly with toy cars then let him do that too. It doesn't matter so long as he has fun and learns things and forms relationships with others, both heterosocial and homosocial.

But once he is a man Gerald will have a choice: Male Invert or Transwoman. Only he can make that choice. And he should be empowered to make it on his own, but with plenty of support and information. Maybe he will make such a choice earlier on, who knows. But the thing is, he should be left to decide for himself in his own time. Maybe he will figure himself out when he's 14, or maybe not until he's 21. But it's his decision and he should be helped to make an informed and independent choice. It has to come from him, and him alone in his own time and on his own terms. He would need space and support, not guidance. That's what I'm trying to say.

Spaces, Groups – And The Community of Women

Should Transwomen be allowed into female only groups, or female only spaces (groups and spaces segregated by sex)?

It is not for me to say, I am a man

It's a women's issue and I'm not a woman

But as a man I am happy to accept Transmen into male only groups and spaces

Only The Community of Women may decide if a Transwomen can enter female-only groups or spaces

The way I see it, Transwomen can only enter female only groups and spaces with The Community of Women's permission – they cannot just invite themselves into them and they have no entitlement which stems from their sex presentation, them doing that has to be cool with The Community of Women for it to be permissible

And The Community of Women can only consist of female humans, people who are biologically female – people who are XX

Female humans need their own group to be with and to represent them. Female humans have unique needs, interests, and concerns. They need their own women-only community. To deny them this would be to liquidate the Community of Women. It would be the abolition of sisterhood. As they have their own sectional interests. Such as safety from male sexual aggression and the fear of male sexual aggression.

But of course, they may accept transwomen into their space and groups if they want to.

However, their decision is final, and they don't have to justify themselves to anyone. If they say "no" then no. If they say "yes" then yes. Calling them horrible names and getting upset is childish, and people to whom they say "no" have zero right to be offended and no right to complain.

If you want everyone to treat you as though you were a woman, then going against The Community of Women and pissing them off is probably not a good move

So, with regards to Transwomen in the women's toilets – whether or not they can be there is up to

The Community of Women – and I believe that their rulings should be enforced.

As a man, whom The Community of Women choose to include or exclude from Female (note: not feminine) spaces and groups is none of my business. And I will always respect and honour the judgments of The Community of Women. It's their decision and I will always abide by whatever they decide.

Here's a thought: *Some women's groups are based on Social Womanhood and others on Biological Womanhood. I think that allowing transwomen into Social Womanhood groups and spaces is different to allowing them into Biological Womanhood groups.*

The knitting club and the female changing rooms are different kinds of Female group/space, that's what I'm saying so perhaps what goes for one needn't go for the other? I don't know and as a Male it is none of my business!

I believe in treating people as individuals. As a member of The Community of Men I am happy to allow Transmen into male-only spaces and groups. But the point is, I have every right not to. I don't exercise that right. But I do maintain it.

As a member of The Community of Men, I am trans-inclusive.

But in saying that I am not saying that individual women or The Community of Women as a whole should be too, just because I personally – one individual male who represents only themselves – happens to feel that way!

On The Importance of Treating People As Individuals

I believe in treating people as individual human beings

And I treat individuals holistically: their mind, their body, their soul

I understand people's humanity through those three things. How clever and skilled they are, what type of body do they have, and whether or not they are good person

I imagine it as being like a triangle, with each factor relating and connecting to the other factors

A kind of Trinity Of The Self?

Those are the three way in which I think of other people, and I'd say that the least important of those is the body

Although yes, your body determines your fate. If you have a diabetic body, then you may need to take Metformin or even insulin. If you have a spinal injury you may need to get around in a wheelchair and if your eyes make you short-sighted then you may need to wear glasses or contact lenses.

And if your body is male, you may be called up for military service (if your body is also young and fit) and if you are female, you may become pregnant (if you have unprotected sex with a man at the right time)

Look at how men, no matter how gentle and peaceful they are as individuals have been drafted and conscripted into various armies over the past two hundred or so years! They have to put on a uniform and go and kill other men, just because they are men. I'm going to call that out as sexist!

Why should men have to be warriors? I don't want to be a warrior. It should be optional, just as motherhood should be entirely optional. In Greece they have a saying, that the army is for men and motherhood is for women (they have conscription there, I actually owe the Greek army 18 month's conscription. Not going to happen!)

Sure, maybe it did in caveman times things were different. But we are no longer in a state of nature and by now you'd think we'd know better, but obviously not!

I think that out of mind, soul, and body that the body is the easiest to modify. It has no will of its own, it is just a lump of oxygenated meat that you have to feed and water. I think that with a soul things are fixed, one is either good or evil, or somewhere in between. And when it comes to the mind some things are more fixed than others. But it is possible to embark upon a journey of self-improvement and to systematically change how your brain works.

When I did my psychology module a key concept in that course was the notion of "Fixity" vs. "Change" in mental states

Here's the thing: It is the mind and the soul who are masculine or feminine and the body who is male or female! – and people are trinities – mind, soul, and body.

And, as Foucault said, "the mind is the prisoner of the body". As too is the soul. But maybe that's a bit pessimistic? – but yes, the social status of the individual (mind/soul) is strongly determined by the societal status of the body.

People should be treated as individuals when it comes to considerations of gender traits, sex presentation, and the credentials of segregation. It should not be a case of "one size fits all".

That is too ridged and ignores the fact that every human situation is different from others.

For instance, the Community of Women would be entitled to let John join the knitting club but not Dave, if they didn't like Dave for whatever reason or want the pleasure of his company.

Basically: take it on a case-by-case basis. That considers each person as a unique individual. As opposed to members of some group or category.

The Idea of "An Invert": A Table And A Graph

They say a picture can say a thousand words…

Here is a diagram to illustrate the idea of "inverts":

	Male	**Female**
Masculine	Man	Female Invert or Transman
Feminine	Male Invert or Transwoman	Woman

Men can be either Men, Male Inverts or Transwomen, and Women can be either Women, Female Inverts, or Transmen

These are the two main choices available for feminine males who want to belong to a category of humans that matches their own nature, their own qualities:

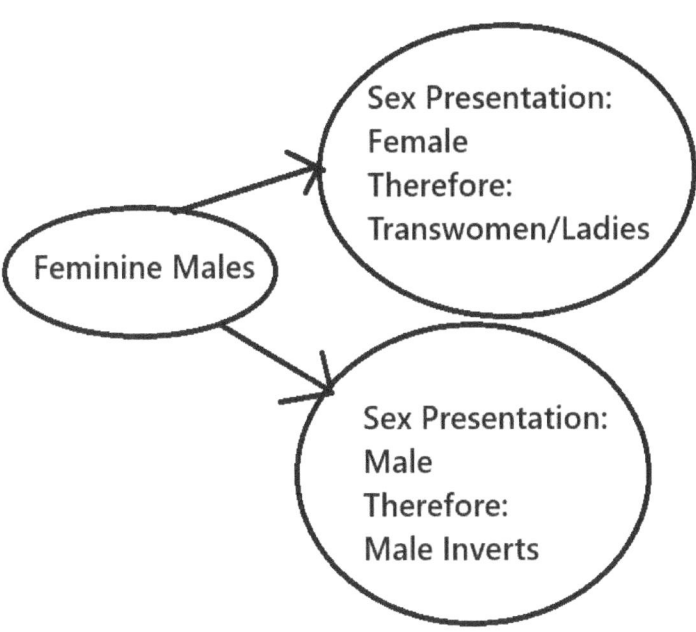

I believe that feminine males have three options: they can either become Transwomen by presenting as women (in which case I would refer to them as being Transwomen) or become Male Inverts (by presenting as males). Or remain in a state of unresolved Gender Dysphoria, being unfulfilled and miserable!

The only real difference is Sex Presentation. That's how Transwomen and Male Inverts differ. Apart from that, they are very similar groups of people.

But yes, it is a BIG difference.

They are different ways of proceeding.

Some feminine males will be happy being Transwomen, and being Transwomen can be the best for some! – I've heard of "gender euphoria" which Transwomen report as having feelings of, having made the leap and gone Trans, to align how they present to the world with their true self. That is totally valid and all power to them.

In exchange, I think the path of the Male Invert should be acknowledged as legitimate.

They are different identity responses to the same situation!

And of course – there is a third option. "Don't Do Anything" and just carry on. But I don't think that's wise, as it basically feminine males living as something they are not – a masculine man. But if people in that position don't want to do anything about it then that's up to them and is legitimate, although I should think they would probably be happier either as a Transwoman or a Male Invert.

And I am aware that alternative gender identities may seem bizarre and weird if you were socialised into the traditional gender paradigm. I think the traditional gender paradigm is like a prison, locking people up from becoming their true authentic selves. Especially when coupled with homophobia and certain traditional notions of masculinity.

I am happy to be in the same category as Transwomen and am happy to embrace them as my sisters. I consider their choices – the way they deal with Gender Dysphoria – to be valid for them, even though it is not for me and indeed not for everybody. And I expect the same in return.

I offer tolerance and acceptance, and I expect that in return.

I understand that although it doesn't make sense for me that doesn't mean it doesn't make sense for others. Yet I maintain that the decision as to how one should present ones sex **can only be made by an adult** and should never be made on behalf of another person.

We should not force girly boys like Gerald to stop being girly, and we should not try and turn him into a girl. Both of those courses of action are wrong and there is zero reason for Gerald to ever feel confused, conflicted, or disordered.

We have the traditional gender paradigm to thank for that, and the liberal paradigm doesn't make the situation much better either…

I believe that Transwomen and Male Inverts should be friends and allies, and I would hate to see some kind of rivalry break out between the two groups. It's not a competition!

I would however like "Male Invert" and "Female Invert" to be both added to the list of LGBTQI identities. The "I" in LGBTQI stands for "Intersex" so why not add another "I" to stand for "Inverts"? – the LGBTQII community! – although yes, that looks like LGBTQ followed by the roman numerals for the number two, so perhaps that could cause problems!

My Own Identity

I am most decidedly a Male Invert.

But I also like the notion of "non-binary", that sounds good to me, that sounds like something I could explore

Perhaps another way of putting it would be "a male non-binary person who presents as masculine"? – but to me that feels a bit messy, and I think "Male Invert" is much better and says a lot more

And "non-binary" sounds a little indecisive, a little uncommitted to me!

I have never been able to play football, I can't throw a punch, I find weight-lifting boring, I don't like risk-taking, I'm frightened of motorcycles, am not super-competitive – I'm just not at all manly. I would be useless in a fight. But none of that makes me a woman!

I am a (mostly) Androphile Male Invert. And I engage in both Heterosocial and Homosocial friendships.

To me, being Trans would open up more problems than it would solve. And I could never pass as a woman. Never. And there are scumbags out there who attack people who are different, I would not want to walk about with an enormous target on my back.

Sure, it shouldn't be that way. But it is. If I to step out in public in wearing (for instance) a dress I would feel highly visible and highly vulnerable. I would be on edge, almost in a state of panic. I would hate it. And it's not as if that's my true self either, because being feminine does not necessitate adopting a feminine appearance, of presenting as Female.

I have a tremendous respect for Trans people who go about presenting as the sex they want to present as. That takes real guts. And I do worry for them. Especially the Transwomen who are clearly male.

But in my case, it is not the fear I have of doing that that is the decisive factor. The decisive factor is that I am not a Transwoman, I am a Male Invert. If I was a Transwoman I'd be calling myself something other than Ed. Not necessarily Edwina, but some other name.

If you think you're a Transwoman then go ahead and do that. I on the other hand am going to go and be a Male Invert. See you at the next pride event!

Masculinity For Male Inverts

Although I identify more with femininity I am undoubtedly male.

The word "Masculinity" has two senses:
　　1. Being Male (sex)

2. Being like how Males are in your given culture (gender)

So for me, I am certainly masculine in the first sense.

And in the other sense yes, I am kind of like that too. As I dress masculine. Like how the menfolk dress. But I think I am also Feminine, in some regards.

It's complicated!

I equate my masculinity as being a member of The Community of Men

Which I believe disqualifies me from The Community of Women

I am very much a member of The Community of Men – it's the only sex-based community I could ever join

I very often feel ashamed of the conduct of some of the members of The Community of Men and there are large toxic and abhorrent male groups, who (sadly) are very much parts of The Community of Men

But I will not mention them here. My point is, that I am critical of how a lot of masculinity exists. And as I said before, there are competing versions of masculinity that all go under the umbrella of The Community of Men, as they are all communities of men! – in my previous example I contrasted the Jocks and the Nerds in American High School dramas.

Anyway, like The Community of Women, The Community of Men is fractured and diverse. And when it comes to trans inclusion, rulings will be different between different individuals, different groups. But if you're male and want to join Female Group A then you need to sort that with the women involved in Female Group A, not those only involved in Group B, or C. So what goes in one setting, with one group of women, may not go in another setting, with another group of women. And the same goes for The Community of Men.

As a man, whatever I do is a form of Masculinity – even if that involves being Feminine!

And I think that is a little absurd, but there you go!

The more you think about its many intricacies, the more complex it feels and the less it makes sense – why do we let such messy things have so much power over people????

My way of being Masculine, of living as a man, is to do so in a way that involves identifying with Femininity!

Male Inverts are men, and "Male Invert" is a masculinity (as it is a way of being a man) but we live as men in Feminine ways.

There should be no compulsion for men to be Masculine but sadly there is, there is a huge amount of pressure on people and very often it is impossible for men to live as Male Inverts – let alone Transwomen.

In some societies Masculinity is not optional. And of course, it should be.

People should be free to be as Masculine or as Feminine as possible

Just as people should be free to present as either Male or Female

Sadly, in perhaps most of the world these freedoms are forbidden, and people are not free to be individuals, to live their lives as they want and to become the type of person they truly are.

In the West, we often take such freedoms for granted. *In most of the world people are not free to base their social identity on their personal identity in the way we can.*

And that's the freedom we're talking about: **Being free to make your social identity match up to your personal identity**

And having the same rights and freedoms as everyone else.

Basically, a big part of being free to be able to be your own authentic self and not having to be anything you're not.

If you want to see how free a society is, see how free you'd be to be yourself, that'll give you a good idea.

My Dating Pool

I am mostly attracted to men, but am a bit attracted to women. I wouldn't go as far to say that I'm bisexual, but I am predominately homosexual

I take people as individuals, that is very important to me

I don't know if I would date Transwomen or Transmen, I don't really know my feelings about doing that

Maybe that would depend on the individuals? I don't know and it doesn't matter.

I've given up on dating anyway.

Human Liberation

I believe that the identity of Invert (both male and female) could liberate and empower a great many people and help people who are not in a good place.

It could help a great many real life people sort out their lives and help them on their quest to develop and grow into a real authentic human being.

That is my main motivation in writing this book (other than sorting out my own head) – to lend a hand to people who are different.

I believe that the meaning of life is to cultivate a well-rounded and happy individuality. I believe this book and the concept of "inverts" could help this a lot.

Invert Pride?

Someone needs to invent a Male Invert Pride flag – and also a Female Invert Pride flag!

Or maybe just an Invert Pride flag – for both Male Inverts and Female Inverts?

I don't know what colours it would have, but they would have to symbolise something, and any such flag would I think need to be based around stripes of some sort!

I have no idea about colours maybe someone out there has?

A New Regime?

This book was originally called "A New Gender Regime"

It basically still proposes that, but does so through a personal exposition of what it means to be a Male Invert

The actual aim of the book is for me to offer my own personal perspective on gender identity and sex in society. And I think I have done that.

Hopefully some of the ideas that were in my brain have travelled into your brain, via whatever medium you have read my words in!

Hopefully all this will help others who are struggling with questions about who and what they are.

I would very much love for people to find this book a helpful resource and I believe that its message could help change society for the better.

And I hope it will be useful and of interest to parents of children such as Gerald.

If lots and lots of people began identifying as either Male or Female Inverts then the entire map of gender relations and sexuality would be re-drawn

And society's gender regime would shift

I've provided the framework; I hope others will join me in a Male and Female Invert movement, which I would like to see included under the LGBT umbrella

I think Male Invert and Female Invert are credible and legitimate gender identities, but I have no idea how many such people there are out there, but the thing is, the concept itself is not really out there, but I know there are lots of feminine males and masculine females who may be interested

This is not a thing that any one person can do on their own!

Thank you for reading.

Just over 24,000 words. Well done!

www.ingramcontent.com/pod-product-compliance
Lightning Source LLC
Chambersburg PA
CBHW031151160426
43193CB00008B/324